Prayer Journal for Kids

A Guide to Heart2Heart Conversations with God

COLEEN M. VEINEER-MCINTOSH

authorHOUSE

AuthorHouse™
1663 Liberty Drive
Bloomington, IN 47403
www.authorhouse.com
Phone: 833-262-8899

Published by AuthorHouse   04/19/2022

ISBN: 978-1-6655-5015-4 (sc)
ISBN: 978-1-6655-5014-7 (e)

Print information available on the last page.

This book is printed on acid-free paper.

Dedication

To my son
Romario you are God's special gift to me.
Thanks for your uplifting words, you encourage
Me to soar like an eagle.
I love you with my whole heart. -Mom

Acknowledgements

First, thank you Lord, for teaching me how to have "heart2heart conversations with you.

Seeking your kingdom first, submitting to your holy training and leading has great rewards and has benefited me.

Use me for your glory.

Special thanks to both my biological and spiritual parents and mentors, who were God appointed.

You have been instrumental in my spiritual growth.

Thank you for allowing God to use you to prepare me for His divine will and purpose for my life.

My Prayer Journal

Dear God:

(Heart2Heart with God -sharing what's on my mind today)

Daily Devotional Reading: *(Subscribe to a 1–3-year bible reading plan) Select/write a focus verse from today's reading.*

Real life application:*(Example of how this verse applies to my life)*

Refection: Listen – What God's holy spirit placed on my heart during our heart2heart conversation today. (Write/Draw)

My Prayer List

List of people I am praying for, and their prayer needs

__My Family

__My Community

__My Country

__The World (global)

1. _____ _____

2. _____

3. _____

4. _____

Thanksgiving reports/Answered Prayers/Testimonies (Write/draw)

My Prayer Journal

Dear God:
(Heart2Heart with God -sharing what's on my mind today)

Daily Devotional Reading: *(Subscribe to a 1–3-year bible reading plan) Select/write a focus verse from today's reading.*

Real life application*:(Example of how this verse applies to my life)*

Refection: Listen – What God's holy spirit placed on my heart during our heart2heart conversation today. (Write/Draw)

My Prayer List

List of people I am praying for, and their prayer needs

___My Family

___My Community

___My Country

___The World (global)

1. _____ _____

2. _____

3. _____

4. _____

Thanksgiving reports/Answered Prayers/Testimonies (Write/draw)

My Prayer Journal

Dear God:

(Heart2Heart with God -sharing what's on my mind today)

Daily Devotional Reading: *(Subscribe to a 1–3-year bible reading plan) Select/write a focus verse from today's reading.*

Real life application:*(Example of how this verse applies to my life)*

Refection: Listen – What God's holy spirit placed on my heart during our heart2heart conversation today. (Write/Draw)

My Prayer List

List of people I am praying for, and their prayer needs

___My Family
___My Community
___My Country
___The World (global)

1. _____ _____

2. _____

3. _____

4. _____

Thanksgiving reports/Answered Prayers/Testimonies (Write/draw)

My Prayer Journal

Dear God:

(Heart2Heart with God -sharing what's on my mind today)

Daily Devotional Reading: *(Subscribe to a 1–3-year bible reading plan) Select/write a focus verse from today's reading.*

Real life application:*(Example of how this verse applies to my life)*

Refection: Listen – What God's holy spirit placed on my heart during our heart2heart conversation today. (Write/Draw)

My Prayer List

List of people I am praying for, and their prayer needs

__My Family
__My Community
__My Country
__The World (global)

1. _____ _____

2. _____

3. _____

4. _____

Thanksgiving reports/Answered Prayers/Testimonies (Write/draw)

My Prayer Journal

Dear God:
(Heart2Heart with God -sharing what's on my mind today)

Daily Devotional Reading: *(Subscribe to a 1–3-year bible reading plan) Select/write a focus verse from today's reading.*

Real life application:*(Example of how this verse applies to my life)*

Refection: Listen – What God's holy spirit placed on my heart during our heart2heart conversation today. (Write/Draw)

My Prayer List

List of people I am praying for, and their prayer needs

___My Family

___My Community

___My Country

___The World (global)

1. _____ _____

2. _____

3. _____

4. _____

Thanksgiving reports/Answered Prayers/Testimonies (Write/draw)

My Prayer Journal

Dear God:
(Heart2Heart with God -sharing what's on my mind today)

Daily Devotional Reading: *(Subscribe to a 1–3-year bible reading plan) Select/write a focus verse from today's reading.*

Real life application:*(Example of how this verse applies to my life)*

Refection: Listen – What God's holy spirit placed on my heart during our heart2heart conversation today. (Write/Draw)

My Prayer List

List of people I am praying for, and their prayer needs

___My Family
___My Community
___My Country
___The World (global)

1. _____ _____

2. _____

3. _____

4. _____

Thanksgiving reports/Answered Prayers/Testimonies (Write/draw)

My Prayer Journal

Dear God:
(Heart2Heart with God -sharing what's on my mind today)

Daily Devotional Reading: *(Subscribe to a 1–3-year bible reading plan) Select/write a focus verse from today's reading.*

Real life application:*(Example of how this verse applies to my life)*

Refection: Listen – What God's holy spirit placed on my heart during our heart2heart conversation today. (Write/Draw)

My Prayer List

List of people I am praying for, and their prayer needs

__My Family
__My Community
__My Country
__The World (global)

1. _____ _____

2. _____

3. _____

4. _____

Thanksgiving reports/Answered Prayers/Testimonies (Write/draw)

My Prayer Journal

Dear God:
(Heart2Heart with God -sharing what's on my mind today)

Daily Devotional Reading: *(Subscribe to a 1–3-year bible reading plan) Select/write a focus verse from today's reading.*

Real life application:*(Example of how this verse applies to my life)*

Refection: Listen – What God's holy spirit placed on my heart during our heart2heart conversation today. (Write/Draw)

My Prayer List

List of people I am praying for, and their prayer needs

___My Family

___My Community

___My Country

___The World (global)

1. _____ _____

2. _____

3. _____

4. _____

Thanksgiving reports/Answered Prayers/Testimonies (Write/draw)

My Prayer Journal

Dear God:

(Heart2Heart with God -sharing what's on my mind today)

Daily Devotional Reading: *(Subscribe to a 1–3-year bible reading plan) Select/write a focus verse from today's reading.*

Real life application:*(Example of how this verse applies to my life)*

Refection: Listen – What God's holy spirit placed on my heart during our heart2heart conversation today. (Write/Draw)

My Prayer List

List of people I am praying for, and their prayer needs

___My Family

___My Community

___My Country

___The World (global)

1. _____ _____

2. _____

3. _____

4. _____

Thanksgiving reports/Answered Prayers/Testimonies (Write/draw)

My Prayer Journal

Dear God:

(Heart2Heart with God -sharing what's on my mind today)

Daily Devotional Reading: *(Subscribe to a 1–3-year bible reading plan) Select/write a focus verse from today's reading.*

Real life application:*(Example of how this verse applies to my life)*

Refection: Listen – What God's holy spirit placed on my heart during our heart2heart conversation today. (Write/Draw)

My Prayer List

List of people I am praying for, and their prayer needs

___My Family

___My Community

___My Country

___The World (global)

1. _____ _____

2. _____

3. _____

4. _____

Thanksgiving reports/Answered Prayers/Testimonies (Write/draw)

My Prayer Journal

Dear God:

(Heart2Heart with God -sharing what's on my mind today)

Daily Devotional Reading: *(Subscribe to a 1–3-year bible reading plan) Select/write a focus verse from today's reading.*

Real life application:*(Example of how this verse applies to my life)*

Refection: Listen – What God's holy spirit placed on my heart during our heart2heart conversation today. (Write/Draw)

My Prayer List

List of people I am praying for, and their prayer needs

___My Family
___My Community
___My Country
___The World (global)

1. _____ _____

2. _____

3. _____

4. _____

Thanksgiving reports/Answered Prayers/Testimonies (Write/draw)

My Prayer Journal

Dear God:
(Heart2Heart with God -sharing what's on my mind today)

Daily Devotional Reading: *(Subscribe to a 1–3-year bible reading plan) Select/write a focus verse from today's reading.*

Real life application:*(Example of how this verse applies to my life)*

Refection: Listen – What God's holy spirit placed on my heart during our heart2heart conversation today. (Write/Draw)

My Prayer List

List of people I am praying for, and their prayer needs

__My Family
__My Community
__My Country
__The World (global)

1. _____ _____

2. _____

3. _____

4. _____

Thanksgiving reports/Answered Prayers/Testimonies (Write/draw)

My Prayer Journal

Dear God:
(Heart2Heart with God -sharing what's on my mind today)

Daily Devotional Reading: *(Subscribe to a 1–3-year bible reading plan) Select/write a focus verse from today's reading.*

Real life application:*(Example of how this verse applies to my life)*

Refection: Listen – What God's holy spirit placed on my heart during our heart2heart conversation today. (Write/Draw)

My Prayer List

List of people I am praying for, and their prayer needs

__My Family
__My Community
__My Country
__The World (global)

1. _____ _____

2. _____

3. _____

4. _____

Thanksgiving reports/Answered Prayers/Testimonies (Write/draw)

My Prayer Journal

Dear God:

(Heart2Heart with God -sharing what's on my mind today)

Daily Devotional Reading: *(Subscribe to a 1–3-year bible reading plan) Select/write a focus verse from today's reading.*

Real life application:*(Example of how this verse applies to my life)*

Refection: Listen – What God's holy spirit placed on my heart during our heart2heart conversation today. (Write/Draw)

My Prayer List

List of people I am praying for, and their prayer needs

___My Family
___My Community
___My Country
___The World (global)

1. _____ _____

2. _____

3. _____

4. _____

Thanksgiving reports/Answered Prayers/Testimonies (Write/draw)

My Prayer Journal

Dear God:

(Heart2Heart with God -sharing what's on my mind today)

Daily Devotional Reading: *(Subscribe to a 1–3-year bible reading plan) Select/write a focus verse from today's reading.*

Real life application:*(Example of how this verse applies to my life)*

Refection: Listen – What God's holy spirit placed on my heart during our heart2heart conversation today. (Write/Draw)

My Prayer List

List of people I am praying for, and their prayer needs

__My Family

__My Community

__My Country

__The World (global)

1. _____ _____

2. _____

3. _____

4. _____

Thanksgiving reports/Answered Prayers/Testimonies (Write/draw)

My Prayer Journal

Dear God:

(Heart2Heart with God -sharing what's on my mind today)

Daily Devotional Reading: *(Subscribe to a 1–3-year bible reading plan) Select/write a focus verse from today's reading.*

Real life application:*(Example of how this verse applies to my life)*

Refection: Listen – What God's holy spirit placed on my heart during our heart2heart conversation today. (Write/Draw)

My Prayer List

List of people I am praying for, and their prayer needs

___My Family

___My Community

___My Country

___The World (global)

1. _____ _____

2. _____

3. _____

4. _____

Thanksgiving reports/Answered Prayers/Testimonies (Write/draw)

My Prayer Journal

Dear God:

(Heart2Heart with God -sharing what's on my mind today)

Daily Devotional Reading: *(Subscribe to a 1–3-year bible reading plan) Select/write a focus verse from today's reading.*

Real life application:*(Example of how this verse applies to my life)*

Refection: Listen – What God's holy spirit placed on my heart during our heart2heart conversation today. (Write/Draw)

My Prayer List

List of people I am praying for, and their prayer needs

__My Family
__My Community
__My Country
__The World (global)

1. _____ _____

2. _____

3. _____

4. _____

Thanksgiving reports/Answered Prayers/Testimonies (Write/draw)

My Prayer Journal

Dear God:
(Heart2Heart with God -sharing what's on my mind today)

Daily Devotional Reading: *(Subscribe to a 1–3-year bible reading plan) Select/write a focus verse from today's reading.*

Real life application:*(Example of how this verse applies to my life)*

Refection: Listen – What God's holy spirit placed on my heart during our heart2heart conversation today. (Write/Draw)

My Prayer List

List of people I am praying for, and their prayer needs

___My Family
___My Community
___My Country
___The World (global)

1. _____ _____

2. _____

3. _____

4. _____

Thanksgiving reports/Answered Prayers/Testimonies (Write/draw)

My Prayer Journal

Dear God:
(Heart2Heart with God -sharing what's on my mind today)

Daily Devotional Reading: *(Subscribe to a 1–3-year bible reading plan) Select/write a focus verse from today's reading.*

Real life application:*(Example of how this verse applies to my life)*

Refection: Listen – What God's holy spirit placed on my heart during our heart2heart conversation today. (Write/Draw)

My Prayer List

List of people I am praying for, and their prayer needs

__My Family
__My Community
__My Country
__The World (global)

1. _____ _____

2. _____

3. _____

4. _____

Thanksgiving reports/Answered Prayers/Testimonies (Write/draw)

My Prayer Journal

Dear God:
(Heart2Heart with God -sharing what's on my mind today)

Daily Devotional Reading: *(Subscribe to a 1–3-year bible reading plan) Select/write a focus verse from today's reading.*

Real life application*:(Example of how this verse applies to my life)*

Refection: Listen – What God's holy spirit placed on my heart during our heart2heart conversation today. (Write/Draw)

My Prayer List

List of people I am praying for, and their prayer needs

___My Family
___My Community
___My Country
___The World (global)

1. _____ _____

2. _____

3. _____

4. _____

Thanksgiving reports/Answered Prayers/Testimonies (Write/draw)

My Prayer Journal

Dear God:

(Heart2Heart with God -sharing what's on my mind today)

Daily Devotional Reading: *(Subscribe to a 1–3-year bible reading plan) Select/write a focus verse from today's reading.*

Real life application:*(Example of how this verse applies to my life)*

Refection: Listen – What God's holy spirit placed on my heart during our heart2heart conversation today. (Write/Draw)

My Prayer List

List of people I am praying for, and their prayer needs

___My Family

___My Community

___My Country

___The World (global)

1. _____ _____

2. _____

3. _____

4. _____

Thanksgiving reports/Answered Prayers/Testimonies (Write/draw)

My Prayer Journal

Dear God:
(Heart2Heart with God -sharing what's on my mind today)

Daily Devotional Reading: *(Subscribe to a 1–3-year bible reading plan) Select/write a focus verse from today's reading.*

Real life application:*(Example of how this verse applies to my life)*

Refection: Listen – What God's holy spirit placed on my heart during our heart2heart conversation today. (Write/Draw)

My Prayer List

List of people I am praying for, and their prayer needs

___My Family

___My Community

___My Country

___The World (global)

1. _____ _____

2. _____

3. _____

4. _____

Thanksgiving reports/Answered Prayers/Testimonies (Write/draw)

My Prayer Journal

Dear God:

(Heart2Heart with God -sharing what's on my mind today)

Daily Devotional Reading: *(Subscribe to a 1–3-year bible reading plan) Select/write a focus verse from today's reading.*

Real life application:*(Example of how this verse applies to my life)*

Refection: Listen – What God's holy spirit placed on my heart during our heart2heart conversation today. (Write/Draw)

My Prayer List

List of people I am praying for, and their prayer needs

___My Family
___My Community
___My Country
___The World (global)

1. _____ _____

2. _____

3. _____

4. _____

Thanksgiving reports/Answered Prayers/Testimonies (Write/draw)

My Prayer Journal

Dear God:
(Heart2Heart with God -sharing what's on my mind today)

Daily Devotional Reading: *(Subscribe to a 1–3-year bible reading plan) Select/write a focus verse from today's reading.*

Real life application:*(Example of how this verse applies to my life)*

Refection: Listen – What God's holy spirit placed on my heart during our heart2heart conversation today. (Write/Draw)

My Prayer List

List of people I am praying for, and their prayer needs

___My Family
___My Community
___My Country
___The World (global)

1. _____ _____

2. _____

3. _____

4. _____

Thanksgiving reports/Answered Prayers/Testimonies (Write/draw)

My Prayer Journal

Dear God:

(Heart2Heart with God -sharing what's on my mind today)

Daily Devotional Reading: *(Subscribe to a 1–3-year bible reading plan) Select/write a focus verse from today's reading.*

Real life application:*(Example of how this verse applies to my life)*

Refection: Listen – What God's holy spirit placed on my heart during our heart2heart conversation today. (Write/Draw)

My Prayer List

List of people I am praying for, and their prayer needs

__My Family

__My Community

__My Country

__The World (global)

1. _____ _____

2. _____

3. _____

4. _____

Thanksgiving reports/Answered Prayers/Testimonies (Write/draw)

My Prayer Journal

Dear God:

(Heart2Heart with God -sharing what's on my mind today)

Daily Devotional Reading: *(Subscribe to a 1–3-year bible reading plan) Select/write a focus verse from today's reading.*

Real life application:*(Example of how this verse applies to my life)*

Refection: Listen – What God's holy spirit placed on my heart during our heart2heart conversation today. (Write/Draw)

My Prayer List

List of people I am praying for, and their prayer needs

___My Family

___My Community

___My Country

___The World (global)

1. _____ _____

2. _____

3. _____

4. _____

Thanksgiving reports/Answered Prayers/Testimonies (Write/draw)

My Prayer Journal

Dear God:
(Heart2Heart with God -sharing what's on my mind today)

Daily Devotional Reading: *(Subscribe to a 1–3-year bible reading plan) Select/write a focus verse from today's reading.*

Real life application:*(Example of how this verse applies to my life)*

Refection: Listen – What God's holy spirit placed on my heart during our heart2heart conversation today. (Write/Draw)

My Prayer List

List of people I am praying for, and their prayer needs

__My Family
__My Community
__My Country
__The World (global)

1. _____ _____

2. _____

3. _____

4. _____

Thanksgiving reports/Answered Prayers/Testimonies (Write/draw)

My Prayer Journal

Dear God:
(Heart2Heart with God -sharing what's on my mind today)

Daily Devotional Reading: *(Subscribe to a 1–3-year bible reading plan) Select/write a focus verse from today's reading.*

Real life application:*(Example of how this verse applies to my life)*

Refection: Listen – What God's holy spirit placed on my heart during our heart2heart conversation today. (Write/Draw)

My Prayer List

List of people I am praying for, and their prayer needs

___My Family

___My Community

___My Country

___The World (global)

1. _____ _____

2. _____

3. _____

4. _____

Thanksgiving reports/Answered Prayers/Testimonies (Write/draw)

About the Author

Coleen M Veineer-McIntosh, MA- Educational Psychology
Currently works as an On-Call, Crisis Service Clinician, where she trains, mentors, coaches, and supervises volunteers who answer calls on the crisis/suicide prevention lines from, youths and adults. Coleen has worked in early childhood education for over twelve years as a Pre-Kindergarten teacher and afterschool/Summer camp program assistant. She has also worked as a sexual assault/domestic violence advocate, and a teen crisis counselor. Coleen currently serves in her local church as a youth sabbath school teacher, Pathfinder co-instructor and children's ministries coordinator. Additionally, she volunteers with community organizations who serve low-income households to teach children and teens about personal finance through her "Financial Literacy for Kid$" workshop. Coleen has an athletic young adult son Romario, who is a college sophomore pursuing his bachelor's in public health/Social Work. Coleen enjoys spending time in the presences of God, worshiping Him through dance, studying His word, praying, fasting, and journaling, as well as gardening, walking on the beach and watching the sunrise, reading, hiking, watching TV (Law and order, NCIS, CSI, Christian movies, shows, and comedies. Top of her list is spending time with her son and Mom. Coleen is honored and passionate to serve children by teaching them about God and helping them to connect with Him in a meaningful way through prayer journaling, poetry, dance and drama.